THE LONDON FILE

PAPERS FROM THE INSTITUTE OF EDUCATION

WHAT WE KNOW ABOUT EFFECTIVE PRIMARY TEACHING

DR. CAROLINE GIPPS

INSTITUTE OF
EDUCATION
UNIVERSITY OF LONDON

Published by

the Tufnell Press

THE LONDON FILE - PAPERS FROM THE INSTITUTE OF EDUCATION

PUBLISHED
by
the Tufnell Press
47, Dalmeny Road, London, N7 0DY

First published   April 1992
Reprinted   January 1993
                   January 1994

BRITISH LIBRARY CATALOGUING-IN-PUBLICATION DATA
A catalogue record for this book is available from the British Library

ISBN 1 872767 16 8

Book design by Fiona Barlow, Carter Wong, London
Printed in Great Britain by Da Costa Print, London

CONTENTS

Introduction

Primary education stands at a water-shed with the National Curriculum increasing the breadth and depth of what must be taught beyond many teachers' felt competence; national assessment and its changing requirements altering profoundly many teachers' understanding of and interaction with assessment; calls from ministers to move away from 'topic teaching' towards formal class teaching; and suggestions from the National Association of Head Teachers (NAHT) that teaching for ten and eleven year olds be subject-specialist based on a secondary model. It seems therefore that this is an appropriate time to take stock and look at what we know about effective primary teaching.

Although there appears to be little consensus, within or outside the profession, about appropriate teaching methods, we do in fact have a fairly clear picture from research on classroom practice. What I want to do in this paper is to cull from theory and from research on practice what it is we know about good primary teaching. What is it that we know and what would a model of primary practice be? This is a crucial question which will not disappear simply because we have a common national curriculum, as the recent 'debate' has shown: a national curriculum, after all, needs a method of 'delivery'.

The Contribution of Theory and Theorists

Traditionally, primary education has looked to child development and psychology for theoretical guidance and underpinning.

Probably the most famous psychologist as far as education is concerned is Piaget. His work has had an enormous influence on primary education, some of it in retrospect, undesirable. Piaget's model is one in which the child develops thought through interaction with the environment. It is now widely accepted that Piaget underestimated the role of language in learning and overestimated the role of play; Barbara Tizard, for example, maintains that one result of this is large open plan nurseries, so that children can have free access to a range of activities, when in fact what they need is sustained conversation with an interested adult (Tizard and Hughes, 1984). The other relevant aspect of Piaget's model is that children go through stages of intellectual development; this was widely interpreted as meaning that it is not possible to teach young children some things until they are 'ready' i.e. that there are limits to their capacity to learn; the corollary of this is that certain concepts emerge spontaneously and by implication cannot be taught (Walkerdine 1984). Though disputed by Bruner, who made the now famous statement that it is possible to teach children anything at any stage in an intellectually honest way, this element of Piaget's work has left us with a legacy, as Alexander (1984) and others have argued, of low expectations for primary aged children.

Piaget's positive contribution, however, was both to start a theoretical debate about young children's intellectual development and to encourage the close observation of children. Thus for example the work of Margaret Donaldson (1978) – who tested Piaget's model by observing children and reworking his experiments – shows us how what is important in the child's performance of a task is, not only his or her stage of development, but also how the task makes sense to the child, and his or her perception of the sort of answer the adult wants. Both these factors have been shown to be central to children's performance in the classroom, as the next section will show.

Bruner, another psychologist of crucial importance for primary education, considered the question: what is it that makes school learning so difficult? His answer was that it is because it is separated from children's real lives and so he incorporated into his theory of learning children's understanding of the situations in which they are asked to perform or learn (Bruner, 1966). For Bruner the essence of learning is that individuals actively select, retain and transform information to a psychological frame of reference (that is, an internal model or system of representation on the basis of which we understand the world). He also sees learning as taking place through interaction with an interested adult and, as children get older, through texts.

Bruner's theory of learning is essentially a 'constructivist' one. Constructivist models of learning assume that knowledge is built up by the child in the form of connected schemata; the child is seen as an agent in his or her own learning actively constructing knowledge. In this model, what is 'taught' to the child is only one of the factors which influence what children learn. By contrast, at the opposite extreme, is the 'transmission' model of learning in which the assumption is that the teacher transmits knowledge or information to the student; the child is seen as an empty vessel, a recipient of information, and children learn what they are taught. The model of learning which we hold has profound implications for how we teach. The latter model is linked with more formal didactic teaching methods and the former with more open and active teaching methods. Constructivist models are currently generally accepted as being more appropriate and of course there are a range of positions along the continuum.

While constructivist views of learning may be in vogue it has proved difficult to develop a pedagogy based on its principles which primary teachers can use consistently successfully with groups of 25-30 children. In the next section I shall describe the progress made by Neville Bennett and Maurice Galton towards framing such a pedagogy.

Vygotsky, the Russian psychologist, has given us a number of crucial insights into how children learn, of which two have particular consequences for classrooms (Vygotsky, 1978). First, that speech in infancy is the direct antecedent of thinking. Very young children discover, so Vygotsky's theory goes, that it is helpful to speak aloud about what they are doing, thus they begin to use 'speech for oneself'. From the ages of 3 to 7 children's speech changes and diversifies so that they develop conversational speech, for communication, in addition to 'speech for oneself'. Piaget's view was that this latter form of speech withers away, while Vygotsky, on the other hand, suggested that this form is internalised, developing into inner speech and eventually into thought. The child then becomes capable of carrying out mental operations more subtle than anything which he or she can put into words (Britton, 1989). As Britton says, if speech in childhood lays the foundations for a lifetime of thinking the implication for pedagogy is enormous, and talking should have a major role in classroom life particularly at infant level.

The second key feature of Vygotsky's theory is that of the 'zone of proximal development'. This refers to the gap that exists for children between what they can do alone and what they can do with help from someone more knowledgeable or skilled than themselves. Here of course the role of the teacher is crucial in the case of young children, and co-operative activity or peer tutoring additionally for older children. The teacher's role then is to make the classroom as rich an interactive learning community as she or he can (Britton *op. cit.*) and through language to lead children into new zones of proximal development (Edwards & Mercer, 1989). Another implication from Vygotsky's model of the zone of proximal development is to do with match: Vygotsky's model would suggest that not all tasks should be perfectly matched to the child's current level of development and skill. Quite the reverse in fact, that some tasks need to be able to shift the child into the next zone *but* what is crucial to this idea is that interaction with another person is required – whether teacher or peer – to help in this moving-on process.

The 'social' constructivist model of learning (see Wood, 1988 and Pollard, 1990) sees children as social beings who construct their understandings from social interaction within the dynamics and constraints of the contexts in which learning takes place. This model focuses on the importance of the degree of control which the learner has over the process of constructing meaning. However, it also recognises the importance of the adult as an agent in the learning process – helping the child to 'make sense' and to move to the next zone of development.

From social psychology we can make use of attribution theory (Gammage, 1984). The life of the classroom is busy, full of interactions and less systematic than the uninitiated would believe. Attribution theory deals with the way in which we make causal inferences about people and events, in other words, that in the absence of actual knowledge or facts we attribute causes of behaviour, understandings, states etc. to people. Within the classroom, Gammage argues, life is so busy and interactions so numerous that the teacher, who cannot assess the exact psychological characteristics which the child brings to any given task, infers, assumes and makes judgements. Indeed, without this process of attribution teachers could not operate for they would be constantly having to use diagnostic assessments of one sort or another. As human beings we attribute cause and effect, often on the most slender of evidence. Since teachers attribute much to pupils which they cannot directly ascertain they need to be aware that this is what they are doing. Of course, in the absence of diagnosis, particularly in regard to match, sensitive attribution based on sensible awareness, Gammage argues, can be helpful.

Another feature of attribution theory is that people often explain their actions by factors that lie outside their control; this means therefore that they are powerless to effect change. Galton (1990) argues that this is one of the reasons why elements of the 'Plowden model' (DES, 1967) were not taken up. For example, very low levels of adult/child interaction are widely observed in classrooms (but this is the antithesis of what the 'Plowden model' stood for), and are explained by teachers as being due to class size. This of course is beyond the teachers' control. In fact, Galton argues, the low levels of interaction are due to classroom organisation and are well within teachers' control.

Something else we can take from psychology is an understanding that children come to the learning experience with their own individual qualities, experiences, conceptions and mental states. Children differ in their prior learning and conceptual level, their rate of learning, their motivation, confidence and self esteem: all these affect their ability to do the task, to absorb the information on offer, to learn the concept, to carry out the process. Every teacher knows this to be the case and it is one of the difficulties with the transmission model of learning: children are not identical empty vessels. The adult must understand what the child knows and the level at which she knows it in order to help the child to move on to the next stage. The child must also be interested in and committed to the material if real learning is to take place; first hand experience and involvement are major motivators for learning.

In fact, because teaching takes place in large groups, the ideal of knowing each child's entry characteristics and modifying teaching and the curriculum to suit, or having and using some perception of the child's system of representation (cf. Bruner, 1966) in order to present information in a form likely to be amenable to the child's frame of reference, is clearly not always possible.

But as well as considering the characteristics of the children and the interaction between these and particular learning experiences or subject matter we need to put into the equation the teacher's own style: which subjects does he/she enjoy teaching, feel most confident in teaching and what is his or her preferred teaching style? To assume that there is one best method for all children and all teachers is to underestimate significantly the complexity of the teaching situation and the interactions involved. Clearly at the heart of the educational process lie the teacher, the child and the curriculum.

One of the limitations of relying on theory, or using research which is explicitly theory based, is that such work tends to focus on one part, or aspect, of the thing which is of concern. For example psychology has traditionally focused on children's learning and abilities, social psychology and sociology on the classroom or school, while studies of curriculum areas have concentrated on the subjects or processes taught. In fact, we need to consider all of these, that is, we need to look at children's mental processes in relation to subject matter and the whole learning context.

Another problem with theory in relation to education is that it has not always attempted to understand the daily practice of teachers before going on to make recommendations about that practice (Golby, 1988). It is now more widely accepted that we need to generate educational theory out of good educational practice (e.g. Hirst, 1984) rather than from the foundation disciplines of psychology, philosophy and sociology. The notion of the 'reflective practitioner' is one (Schon, 1983) that is particularly helpful in viewing the relation between theory and practice in teaching. This is not to say that 'outsiders' such as researchers (with a thorough knowledge of teaching and classrooms) cannot observe good practice in action and help to build up a pedagogic theory.

In fact, as both Simon (1981) and Galton (1989) point out, education in this country is characterised by an absence of any serious discussion of pedagogy – the science of teaching – and official documents are characterised by their absence of any theory. Simon considers that one of the manifestations of this was the Schools Council approach to curriculum development and reform which he describes as essentially pragmatic and atheoretical. National curriculum and assessment developments today suffer from a similar lack of theoretical framework or consideration of pedagogy.

One of Simon's key points is that we need to move away from the Plowden view which focused on the individual child and individual differences (a view which Walkerdine also takes, but for different reasons (1984)) because to develop pedagogy we need to start from what children have in common as members of the human species in order to establish the general principles of teaching and then to determine what modifications are needed to meet individual's needs. If the view is that each child requires a specific pedagogical approach, then the construction of general principles of teaching becomes impossible. Simon argues (and research shows) that teachers who set up tasks for individual children then have a complex management problem which takes up all their energies (Simon, 1981 p. 142).

So theory's contribution lies in the insights that it can give us: not for any one theory's ability to give us all, or indeed any, of the right answers, but to offer a range of insights which we can use to build up an understanding of the science *and* art of teaching within the complex classroom setting.

The Contribution of Research

What does research tell us about effective primary teaching?

Neville Bennett, Maurice Galton and colleagues have been researching primary classrooms for over 15 years and their writings are enormously important in the search for a primary pedagogy. Two major research studies carried out in London of junior schools, by Peter Mortimore and colleagues, and of infant schools by Barbara Tizard and colleagues, throw more light on effective teaching and learning. I shall concentrate here on these four researchers and their work.

Bennett's was the first attempt in the post-Plowden era to work towards an effective model of teaching for primary schools. *Teaching*

Styles and Pupil Progress (1976) framed the debate in terms of teachers' styles categorised as formal, informal and mixed. He studied the effect these had on children's performance in Maths and English. This study only looked at fourth year junior teachers and classes, relied mostly on self-report by teachers and did not control for curriculum activity. There were also considerable problems with the design and analysis of the study – perhaps inevitable in the first of a series of studies of this sort, being a major new model.[1]

Bennett concluded that *teachers' style* did make a difference to performance on the tests used, and *time on task* seemed to be an important intervening variable.

The limitations with this approach became evident however (Bennett, 1987) since it did not focus on the pupils (who not only influence their own learning through their interactions with the teacher, but bring their personal and cognitive styles to the classroom) and since this broad classification of teachers was too gross to be meaningful. Bennett's work then moved towards focusing on the pupils' learning experiences (Bennett, et al. 1984). Time on task and 'match' i.e. the matching of level of difficulty of task to the level of attainment of the child, were key issues within what Bennett refers to as the 'opportunity to learn' paradigm. (Bennett, 1987 *op. cit.*). The assumption within this paradigm is that pupil activity is central to the effect of teaching on learning, in other words there is no *direct* relationship between teacher behaviour and pupil achievement since the pupil mediates by his/her activities. The teachers' crucial contribution is in managing the pupils' attention and time.

Bennett concluded that, contrary to the earlier work within this paradigm, time on task was not alone a sufficient condition for learning. Despite the fact that research indicates consistently that length of the school day, the amount of time spent on learning activities and homework all relate to pupil achievement: "There is little to be gained from high pupil involvement on tasks that are either not comprehensible or worthwhile" (Bennett, 1987 *op. cit.*). Thus the *quality and level of the task set* entered the debate.

Unhappily the next study by Bennett, Desforges and colleagues (1984) showed that, even in the classrooms of teachers who were identified as being good class-teachers, only 40 per cent of tasks matched pupils' capabilities. Furthermore the tasks set by the teacher did not always embody their intentions. Now, given that these were experienced, good teachers, we need to consider why the 'match' was poor. This, we cannot fail to notice, is a regular theme of the HMI: they report poor match with an awesome regularity (HMI 1978, 1983, 1985). Desforges and Cockburn (1987) point to the logistics of the teacher's task. We may believe that "the single most important factor influencing learning is what the learner already knows. Ascertain this and teach him accordingly" (Ausubel, 1968), but with a class of 30 pupils if the teacher did nothing else she would have slightly less than 10 minutes a day to focus on each individual child. Given the dynamics of large groups of young children, the fact that the state of children's knowledge is changing all the time, and the number of curriculum areas covered, actually to diagnose correctly on a regular basis the understanding of every child and to set work at an appropriate level is clearly impossible, as Simon pointed out. Thus the teacher must limit her diagnostic activity and aim her teaching (albeit unwittingly) 'down the middle'. So one of the necessary conditions for learning, the appropriate level of the task set, is problematic within large mixed-ability classes.

Bennett's next move was to bring *teachers' subject knowledge* into the arena. How can teachers teach well knowledge which they themselves do not thoroughly understand, how can they identify pupil misconceptions or misunderstandings or make decisions about what counts as development in content areas with which they are not thoroughly conversant? Is teachers' poor subject knowledge part of the problem in lack of diagnosis, which for Bennett means identifying appropriate tasks for children? Findings from this research indicate that only a third of primary teachers feel competent to teach science, 27 per cent to teach music and 14 per cent design and technology in the National Curriculum (Wragg, Bennett and Carré, 1989). Findings which did not bode well for the teaching of some National Curriculum subjects (Bennett and Carré, 1991).

Bennett now concludes that teachers need a range of teaching styles and his current model is one which includes *interactions of teacher, pupil and task within the complex social setting of the classroom.* Here Bennett draws on Doyle's ecological model of the classroom as a complex environment and information system to which teacher and pupil must adapt (Doyle, 1986). "To understand the degree to which teaching prospers learning it is necessary to ascertain the extent to which the intellectual demand in assigned work is appropriate or matched to pupils' capabilities. Further, since classroom learning takes place within a complex social environment it is necessary to understand the impact of social processes on children's task performances" (Bennett, 1988).

The first major study by Maurice Galton and his colleagues, ORACLE (Galton et al., 1980) used systematic classroom observation to study teacher and pupil behaviour in the classroom. What this study showed was that primary teachers were involved in interaction with pupils for nearly 80 per cent of the time they were observed. What was significant, however, was the pattern of these interactions: 70 per cent were with individual children, 20 per cent with the whole class and under 10 per cent with groups. Since there is little group interaction and given the proportion of teachers to children what this interaction pattern means is that for children their main contact with the teacher is when she is interacting with the whole class – this accounted for nearly three quarters of the attention that an individual pupil received from the teacher. Again, because there was little co-operative group work observed, pupils did not interact with other pupils either, thus the interaction pattern for pupils was the opposite of that for teachers, with almost 80 per cent of their

11

time not interacting with anybody. Galton pointed out that the teachers' decision to work with individual children meant that tasks had to be set which did not make too many demands on the teacher hence the widespread use of published schemes and work sheets. This strategy in turn led to a greater emphasis on the traditional areas of the curriculum, or the basics, than was assumed to be the case in the post-Plowden era. Another consequence of this pattern of classroom organisation and the high number of interactions was that the majority were lower-order interactions, that is, to do with organisational matters, giving guidance on routine and factual statements. Nearly 45 per cent of exchanges were teacher statements and there was little discussion, higher order questioning or sustained interaction observed. Another study with a slightly different time sampling observation technique, indicated that the interactions with individual pupils were short (i.e. a high proportion of interactions were with a different pupil five seconds later) thus giving little opportunity to engage in challenging discussion which of necessity requires sustained interaction (Galton, 1989). This picture again does not fit with the assumed post-Plowden picture of the modern primary classroom, based on questioning, discovery methods and group activities.

Galton and colleagues also classified their teachers into types and investigated pupils' progress in relation to these types. What this part of the research indicated was that two groups of teachers were more successful. The first group were those who were able to sustain high levels of questioning, eliciting factual information and challenging responses from the children and providing feedback to the pupils about their work. They made conscious switches of strategy from class to individual teaching in order to maintain their desired pattern of teaching tactics. The second group was those who worked with the class as a whole regularly and had the highest level of challenging questions, cultivated a positive climate in the classroom by using praise more often than other teachers, often demonstrated tasks and showed things to the whole class so that the children were to an extent learning by example.

What comes through again and again from Galton's work is the importance of *high levels of questioning* and the need to engage in strategies which allow *maximum levels of sustained interaction* with all pupils. This is a finding which has been replicated in the ILEA Junior School Study (see below), and would of course be consistent with Vygotsky's theory. Wood (1988) however, shows how too much teacher questioning is 'closed' and leads to low-level responses from the children. What raises the level of response is offering a longer response time (which many teachers find difficult) or teacher input which is high in cognitive level itself, e.g. offering speculations, hypotheses and conjectures; this stimulates more talk, questions and ideas from pupils and generates discussion between them.

Galton also discusses children's own contribution to poor match. During the later stages of the ORACLE work (Delamont and Galton, 1986, and Galton, 1987) – Galton used informal qualitative observations and interviews with pupils to help explain the quantitative data. He concluded that pupils are anxious to please the teacher and to do what she wants, so they find high-risk situations (e.g. being called upon to answer questions) threatening. They thus attempt to avoid being picked on to answer questions, or to get the teacher to give as many clues as possible until the 'correct' answer is framed for them. Galton maintains that pupils offer good behaviour and a reasonable amount of work in exchange for tasks which have low ambiguity and are well within their capability, so that they do not have to expose their ignorance to the class or the teacher (see also Holt, 1984). Work by Pollard further suggests that the children are trying to maintain good relationships with their peers while at the same time coping with shared social understandings of routines, conventions and expectations, (Pollard, 1987). Galton argues that in some classroom settings children develop a variety of strategies to slow down their work rate. For example, faced with the possibility that completing one work sheet will ensure another containing more difficult examples pupils, understandably, prefer to take as long as possible to complete the first one (Galton, 1989 p. 118). He suggests that a concerted effort of this kind by a class, particularly during the first few weeks of the school year, creates a situation in which the 'new' teacher expects these children to manage only a certain amount of work during a session. Thus mismatch occurs in that the pupils do not get any quicker when doing practice tasks, and Galton argues that the children have contributed to this mismatch.

Galton concludes that if teachers are to be able to question individual pupils in a sustained way about their work in order to diagnose their learning problems then the children must have independent learning strategies, be less dependent on the teacher and not find the questioning threatening. Galton's view is that children need to have the confidence to think for themselves, and not to be dependent on the teacher if they are to engage in independent learning. However, many teachers exert their authority by using power over the children, particularly when there are conflicts over behaviour. Pupils then conform out of fear (of embarrassment or loss of status and self-esteem). This requires them to be dependent upon the teacher for clues to acceptable behaviour and this dependency is transmitted to their work. Edwards and Mercer (1989 *op. cit.*) argue similarly, that even within a 'Plowden-type discovery' approach children must come up with spontaneous solutions to 'problems' which are at the same time the teachers' solutions. The child tries to discern in the teachers' cues, clues and questions what the required answer is; so the child is not discovering knowledge for herself, it is merely a different way of coming to the teachers' knowledge. This again increases the child's dependence on the teacher and limits their autonomy. Alexander (1991) describes life in Leeds primary classrooms as running on a similar model, with low level questioning and teacher-determined classroom dialogue.

An alternative approach (Galton, 1989) involves an open negotiation between teacher and pupils so that consideration is given within a shared framework of behaviour to both teacher's and pupils' needs. Thus Galton's work, too, now looks at the *interaction between teacher, pupil and task within the complex social setting of the classroom.*

Other research has looked at effective schools rather than effective teachers. Peter Mortimore and colleagues at the then ILEA Research and Statistics Branch, carried out a longitudinal study of 2,000 junior school children in 50 schools. This study was designed to replicate, though in a modified and technically improved way, the secondary school study *Fifteen Thousand Hours*. Both studies had the major aim of investigating the issue of what makes an effective school. The junior school study, published as *School Matters* (Mortimore et al., 1988) collected an enormous amount of data: detailed information about the children's age, social class, sex, race and attainment on entry to school; detailed information about the children's attainment in cognitive and non-cognitive areas in each of the four years of junior school; and detailed evidence about school organisation collected by researchers as well as through questionnaires and self-report by the teachers. This use of more than one technique to look at teaching practice is important since there is often a gap between what teachers do and what they say they do, and equally observers' interpretations of events needs checking with the actors'. Mortimore and colleagues found for example that the majority of teachers reported in interviews that they spent most of their time dealing with the class as a whole rather than with individuals or groups. The observations, however, showed that this was not the case – teachers spent much more time communicating with individual children than with the class or groups.

What the study found was that, once differences in pupil intake were taken into account, some schools were definitely more effective – in terms of pupil progress – than others. Because of the complex nature of the analysis it was possible to identify a range of factors that contributed to this effectiveness.

At the classroom level the effective features were these: teacher responsibility for ordering activities during the day for pupils, that is teachers took the responsibility for structuring the day, facilitating balance and variety; some pupil responsibility for their work and independence *within* sessions; covering only one curriculum area at a time; high levels of interaction with the class as a whole (these two were related); use of higher-order questions and statements (i.e. those which encourage responses which are of an imaginative or problem-solving kind); provision of ample challenging work (which resulted in high levels of pupil involvement); a positive atmosphere in the classroom with high levels of praise and encouragement.

The findings in relation to teachers using higher order questions, giving encouragement and praise and working with the class as a whole in order to maximise and sustain interactions, replicate Galton's findings. Mortimore and colleagues were able to show that for teachers who spent a lot of time on contacts with individual pupils much of this interaction was about routine (i.e. non-work) matters and there was less use of higher order questioning, while teachers who used class discussions as a teaching strategy also tended to make rather more use of higher-order communication. Teachers who used mixed activity sessions and integrated curriculum areas in a topic approach also spent more time on non-work contacts with pupils; these pupils showed higher levels of noise and movement, but also higher levels of inter-pupil co-operation. Mortimore concludes that classroom factors which contribute to effective teaching are: structured sessions, intellectually challenging teaching, a work centred environment, maximum communication between teacher and pupils and a limited focus within sessions. The recent Leeds report (Alexander, 1991) serves to confirm the findings of Galton and Mortimore in this area.

It seems that it is the amount, nature and content of teacher-pupil talk which is crucial to pupil learning and that communicating with groups and the whole class enables more children to experience sustained, higher-order, work-related interactions with the teacher. Focusing on one curriculum activity at a time enables the teacher to raise intellectually challenging points with pupils and class discussions, when handled well, can be challenging and stimulating.

Barbara Tizard and colleagues carried out a similar study in 33 London infant schools (Tizard et al., 1988) trying to find out what it is that schools and teachers contribute to children's progress. A specific focus of their work was, in addition, the differences in performance between boys and girls and the achievement of children of Afro-Caribbean origin. Like the Junior School Study this was longitudinal: it looked at the children's attainment on entry to school, it looked at home and school factors during the infant school years (carrying out observational studies in school and interviewing parents) and measured the children's progress in the basic skills in each of the three years of the study.

Apart from the finding that the strongest predictor of attainment at age seven was the amount of '3R' knowledge the children had even before they started school, Tizard's study showed that there were strong relationships between curriculum coverage, the teachers' expectations of individual children and their progress. Curriculum coverage varied widely among schools and this was also related to progress regardless of teacher expectations: the more the children were exposed to, the more progress they made. When teachers with limited curriculum coverage were asked why they had not introduced certain items to their classes they replied that these things were too difficult for children of that age, or in that school. Yet, as Tizard and colleagues point out, teachers in other schools in the study with children of very similar ability had introduced these items. Classrooms were well-ordered and busy and children did not spend much time in play (14 per cent and 2 per cent of classroom time at reception and top infant respectively) but they also spent very little time actually engaged in reading (only 4 per cent of the working time, i.e. 8 minutes a day approximately, at top infant level) which the researchers cite as the cause of low levels of reading attainment in the schools. Those classes where children were reading for considerably longer were using techniques such as reading to each other or reading in groups rather than always to the teacher individually. Another disquieting finding was that the children spent almost half their school day (43 per cent) on dinner time, playtime, lining-up, register and other non-work activities. A quarter of their time is spent at dinner and in the playground. Less than half the day (46 per cent) was devoted to learning activities in the classroom – of this 64 per cent was spent on the '3Rs'. Overall, children observed were engaged in their tasks 61 per cent of the time. Given the evidence that these were fairly low level, repetitive activities one is amazed at children's ability to stick docilely at the task in hand, although there are echoes of the contract between teacher and children which Galton and Pollard describe: we will behave well and work hard if you give us work that is predictable and easy.

What this study points out, in common with the Junior School Study, is that children need to be exposed to an ample range of challenging and interesting tasks. To summarise, teacher expectation for this sample of inner-city children was, for whole classes, too low; where teachers had higher expectations for individual children they were exposed to a wider range of curriculum and learning experiences; there was wide variation in curriculum coverage and this affected progress; much of the school day was spent on non-work activities; very little of the children's time was spent on reading by the top infant class and this affected progress; there was also very little maths teaching observed in the reception classes of almost all schools. The lack of balance in time spent on various curriculum areas will, of course, be changing with the introduction of the National Curriculum. In the first year of its introduction, however, HMI found many schools were spending a disproportionate amount of time on the core subjects, which caused concern about their ability to devote 'reasonable time' to all National Curriculum subjects (HMI 1989).

Conclusions : looking to the future

What are the conclusions that we can take from this research ? What does it tell us about good primary teaching which can help us to frame an effective pedagogy?

All the evidence points to the fact that when teachers take as their main focus individual children most of their interactions are routine, organisational and low-level; the children, by contrast, get little teacher attention, working mostly on their own. As a result, extended discussions with children about the tasks – including higher-order questions and statements – are severely limited. In order to achieve this sustained interaction more use needs to be made of class and group work. Where classwork is common, this is usually accompanied by a reduction in the amount of subject integration and the integrated day. Indeed, structuring the day for pupils and focusing on one curriculum area at a time were strong factors in effective teaching. So too is the provision of a plentiful and wide range of work tasks, which need to be matched to the child's level of attainment and understanding so that a balance of practice/consolidation tasks and learning/extension tasks is achieved. Important too is a good, positive, atmosphere in the classroom with plenty of encouragement and praise, high levels of expectation for all children and high levels of work-related talk and discussion

What does 'theory' tell us about good teaching? What the 'theorists' tell us is that children are capable of more than we tend to give them credit for, provided that they understand what is required by the task; that interaction with others is of crucial importance as is language; that through language the young child learns, among other things, to think[2]; that through interaction with others children can explore their own knowledge and understand how the new knowledge they are 'learning' fits in with this prior knowledge. But research tells us that the adult-child interactions need to be sustained, challenging and extended rather than fragmented and routine. The picture is thus of classrooms with an emphasis on language and challenge rather than quiet 'busy work'. This picture matches the one provided by research on classrooms and we need to continue to get this message over to teachers.

It is clear then, in our model of good practice, that we need to emphasise strategies for increasing levels of interaction between teachers and children and higher order questions and statements; as Vygotsky and Bruner both point out, the younger the child the more they learn from language and the less from texts. We also need to work on ways of enabling teachers to assess children's levels of understanding or attainment so as to enable tasks to be appropriately matched. The teacher assessment element of National Curriculum assessment, if we can get to a model which is manageable and for which teachers are properly prepared and trained, could be an important element in the 'matching' process. Of course, informal assessment is also the way in which, following constructivist models of learning, one finds out how children think about things before developing those ideas.

Given that in classes of 25-30, teachers cannot match every task to every child's ability one fairly common tactic is to present material and tasks to the class, discuss it altogether so that all children are listening to the teacher and are an audience, if not participants, in the sustained interaction, then for the teacher to go around and modify the task and/or give further explanation to individuals or groups. Another tactic is to develop co-operative or collaborative group work so that children interact with each other, and both Galton and Bennett have turned their attention to this. However, as the ORACLE research showed, children dislike group work because of the high levels of ambiguity and risk perceived in it, so teachers also need to know how to develop a classroom climate in which children have some control over their learning and are not dependent on the teacher so that such situations are not threatening to them. Early results indicate that when co-operative groupwork is facilitated, there are high levels of task-related talk in the group and the demands on the teacher decrease significantly; when interactions do take place they tend to be higher-order rather than routine (Dunne and Bennett, 1990).

Thus we have two strategies – a version of 'traditional' class teaching which is modified around the edges to match some individual needs, and co-operative group work – both of which aim to reduce individual demands on the teacher and allow pupils to engage in increased amounts of task-related interaction. It is also possible that teachers need a mix of approaches to suit their own style and that of the children; just such a range of strategies has been recommended by Alexander, Rose and Woodhead (1992). Classrooms should have a shared responsibility for learning: the teacher structures the session and allocates the task, but the child has responsibility for how the task is carried out and has some responsibility for his or her learning, thus reducing dependency on the teacher (see Yeomans, 1987).

One reality that we need to face is that we will have to work within current, or increased, class size. All teaching would be easier in smaller classes. However, given the likelihood of future problems in teacher supply, it seems unlikely that class size can be expected to decrease in the near future. As Lawton (1990) points out the unhappy coincidence of the increase in primary school pupil numbers (over half a million from 1990 to 2000) combined with the fall in numbers of school leavers during the same decade leading to a diminished pool of young people for teacher training, the lowered status of teaching as a profession and unattractive salary levels compared with other graduate careers, together with the proportion of practising teachers who are leaving the profession,[3] together present a picture of teacher shortages of frightening proportion. This year's improvement in the teacher supply figures seems to be the result of the recession rather than any more positive factors. As Professor Smithers has put it, 'Government has solved the teacher supply crisis by closing down the economy' (TES, 1991).

So, as well as looking for ways of improving the status and morale of the teaching profession and looking at alternative models of training, we will need to cope, certainly in the interim, with current or increased class size. It is clear then that we cannot encourage an approach which focuses mainly or solely on the individual child. One possibility – as well as more classwork and co-operative group work – would be to employ classroom assistants who can take the routine and organisational tasks away from the teacher leaving him/her free to concentrate on work tasks and higher order interactions, assessment and curriculum planning. One version of the two-tier model put forward by Lawton (1990 *op. cit.*) is based on three different levels of qualification, training and experience with initial/licensing trainees, probationer/induction teachers, and those with fully qualified teacher status (perhaps with an MA) all working in classrooms but with clear differences in the roles and tasks which they undertake.

Teachers reading this paper may feel that there has been an undue emphasis on problems and difficulties. There are of course, many effective and exciting schools and teachers, and, at its best, being a primary teacher is extremely satisfying, though demanding. All those who have been in primary classrooms can point to the rewards, excitements and deep satisfaction that working with young children bring. Indeed as Nias' account shows (Nias, 1989) many teachers derive intense satisfaction from feeling natural and whole in their relationship with children and from creating a sense of community within classes and schools. This is not sentimental anecdote, it is part of the long held view of teaching as education, not of teaching as direct instruction. Similarly, Woods' (1987) account of relationships between teachers and children and the caring, friendly and cheerful atmosphere, which is a feature of all good primary schools answers his own question: why do teachers carry on teaching?

We know much about effective teaching strategies, research has done much to show us what these strategies are, while theories have helped us to make sense of the findings. It is important now to make sure that what we know about effective primary teaching does not get lost under the weight of National Curriculum folders, statements of attainment and statements from ministers.

The problem with externally-imposed change is that it devalues people's previous practice – they cannot have been right, otherwise there would be no need to change. In the area of curriculum coverage and match this may have been true for a number of teachers, but it is only part of the picture. Framing the model from a basis of research on good classroom practice should be one element in restoring morale and felt worth for teachers since our information on effective practice has come, as it only can, from observing effective teachers at work.

Notes

1. Although Joan Barker Lunn's earlier work : *Streaming in the Primary School* (1970) also categorised teachers into types on the basis of whether their lessons and attitudes were mostly traditional or progressive.

2. It was Bertrand Russell who said, 'Most people would die sooner than think, and most people do.'

3. Professor Smithers' survey for the Leverhulme Trust indicates that teachers are leaving at about five times the rate of official DES figures (Smithers et al., 1989) and more recently that teacher turnover in London and the South East is worryingly high (Smithers and Robinson, 1991).

Bibliography

Alexander, R. (1984) *Primary teaching*, Holt Reinhardt Winston.

Alexander, R. (1991) *Primary education in Leeds*, University of Leeds.

Alexander, R., Rose, J. and Woodhead, C. (1992) *Curriculum organisation and classroom practice in primary schools*, DES.

Ausubel, D. (1968) *Educational psychology: A cognitive view*, Holt Reinhardt Winston.

Barker Lunn, J. (1970) *Streaming in the primary school*, NFER.

Bennett, N. (1976) *Teaching styles and pupil progress*, Open Books.

Bennett, N. (1987) 'Changing perspectives on teaching learning processes' *Oxford Review of Education* 13,1.

Bennett, N. (1988) 'The effective primary school teacher: The search for a theory of pedagogy' *Teaching and Teacher Education* 4,1.

Bennett, N. et al. (1984) *The quality of pupil learning experiences*, Lawrence Erlbaum.

Bennett, N. and Carré, C. (1991) 'No substitutes for a base of knowledge', *Times Educational Supplement*, 8 November.

Britton, J. (1989) 'Vygotsky's contribution to pedagogical theory' in Murphy, P. and Moon, B. (Eds) *Developments in learning and assessment*, Hodder & Stoughton.

Bruner, J. (1966) *Towards a theory of instruction*, Harvard University Press.

Delamont, S. and Galton, M. (1986) *Inside the secondary classroom*, Routledge & Kegan Paul.

DES, (1967), Department of Education and Science, 'Children at their primary schools', (Plowden Report), HMSO.

Desforges, C. and Cockburn, R. (1987) *Understanding the mathematics teacher*, Falmer.

Donaldson, M. (1978) *Childrens' minds*, Fontana.

Doyle, W. (1986) 'Classroom organisation and management' in M.C. Wittrock (ed.) *Handbook of research on teaching*, New York, Macmillan (3rd ed.).

Dunne, E. and Bennett, N. (1990) *Talking and learning in groups*, Macmillan Education.

Edwards, D. and Mercer, N. (1989) *Common knowledge*, Routledge.

Galton, M. (1987) 'An ORACLE Chronicle: A decade of classroom research' *Teaching and Teacher Education* 3,4.

Galton, M. (1989) *Teaching in the primary school*, David Fulton Publishers.

Galton, M and Simon, B. (1980) *Progress and performance in the primary classroom*, Routledge & Kegan Paul.

Gammage, P. (1984) 'The curriculum and its participants: Perspectives of interaction' in M. Skilbeck (ed.) *Readings in school-based curriculum development*, Paul Chapman Publishing.

Golby, M. (1988) 'Traditions in primary education' in Clarkson, M. (ed.) *Emerging issues in primary education*, Falmer.

Hirst, P. (1984) 'Educational theory' in Hirst, P. ed *Educational theory and its foundation disciplines*, Routledge & Kegan Paul.

HMI (1978) *Primary education in England*, HMSO.

HMI (1983) *9-13 middle schools: An illustrative survey*, HMSO.

HMI (1985) *Education 8-12 in combined and middle schools*, HMSO.

HMI (1989) *The implementation of the National Curriculum in primary schools*, HMSO.

Holt, J. (1984) *How children fail*, Penguin.

Lawton, D. (1990) 'The future of teacher education in England and Wales' paper given to ATEE conference August 1990. In Graves, N. (ed.) *Initial teacher education: Policies and progress*, Kogan Page (London Educational Studies, ULIE).

Mortimore, P. et al. (1988) *School matters: The junior years*, Open Books.

Nias, J. (1989) *Primary teachers talking*, Routledge.

Pollard, A. (ed.) (1987) *Children and their primary schools*, Falmer.

Pollard, A. (1990) 'Towards a sociology of learning in primary schools' *British Journal of Sociology of Education* 11,3.

Schon, D. (1983) *The reflective practitioner*, Temple Smith.

Simon, B. (1981) 'Why no pedagogy in England?' in Simon, B. and Taylor, W. (eds) *Education in the Eighties*, Batsford.

Smithers, A. et al. (1989) *A study of teacher loss*, Leverhulme Trust.

Smithers, A. and Robinson, P. (1991) *Teacher provision*, University of Manchester.

TES (1991) *Times Educational Supplement*, 27 December, 1991.

Tizard, B. and Hughes, M. (1984) *Young children learning*, Fontana.

Tizard, B. et al. (1988) *Young children at school in the inner city*, Lawrence Erlbaum Associates.

Vygotsky, L. (1978) *Mind in society*, Harvard University Press.

Walkerdine, V. (1984) 'Developmental psychology and the child centred pedagogy' in Henriques, J. et al. (eds) *Changing in the subject*, Methuen.

Wood, D. (1988) *How children think and learn*, Blackwell.

Woods, P. (1987) 'Managing the primary teacher's role' in Delamont, S. ed. *The Primary school teacher*, Falmer.

Wragg, E., Bennett, N. and Carré, C. (1989) 'Primary teachers and the National Curriculum' *Research Papers in Education* 4,3.

Yeomans, R. (1987) 'Making the large group feel small' *Cambridge Journal of Education* 17,3.

Changing literacies: Media education and modern culture
David Buckingham

'TV zombies', 'witless media dupes' or techno-whiz-kids? What will changing media technologies make of our children? David Buckingham argues that the proposal to remove media education from the National Curriculum for English ignores the central importance of the media in children's lives and the rise of new forms of technologically inspired literacy. The children in our schools today must inhabit the media-oriented, technical, cultural and literary landscape of the twenty-first century. We must not shrink from providing them with the competence and understanding which will enable them to inhabit this landscape with ease.
ISBN 1 872767 61 3   28 pp   paperback   £3.95

Partnership in teacher training: Talk and chalk
Clare Hake

Learning on the job will not produce teachers who can reflect on, compare, and thereby improve their practice. Clare Hake applauds the recent shift in emphasis towards more school-based teacher training, but argues that university departments of education can and must make a continuing contribution to training. In the space created by a partnership between school and college, students can conduct 'an active and rational exploration of the task of teaching'. Using her own experience first as a mentor for trainee teachers in school, and later as a university curriculum tutor, Clare Hake describes and illustrates the advantages of the partnership between school and college exemplified by the Oxford University teacher training scheme. School experience may be paramount but impoverished without the opportunity for reflection provided by such a partnership.
ISBN 1 872767 46 X   36 pp   paperback   £3.95

A market-led alternative for the curriculum: Breaking the code
James Tooley

The National Curriculum is a national disaster. But there appears to be a consensus that a national curriculum of some kind is desirable. James Tooley challenges this consensus, and argues radically that curricula should be entrusted to the market. Reviewing the arguments for a national curriculum, he concludes that a cumbersome, costly, unreliable and ultimately unnecessary, national system should be abandoned and market forces should be allowed to operate. He argues that a market-led curriculum would be liberating, empowering and facilitate egalitarian ideas far better than any bureaucratised, centralised curriculum.
ISBN 1 872767 51 6   42 pp   paperback   £3.95

Education and the crisis in values: should we be philosophical about it?
Graham Haydon

'Education should seek to impart moral values'—what does this mean? *Does* society face a moral crisis? Does the increasingly public expression of a plurality of moral values signal a decline or an advance? Can education help us with the plurality of values with which we have to live? Graham Haydon addresses these complex issues, arguing that philosophy *can* both help us to understand the current crisis in values and to deal with it. While philosophy may not provide teachers with a lifeline for survival in the classroom, philosophers just might prove to be swimming instructors. Philosophy need not be remote from popular understanding, and should be brought more fully into the training of teachers and into the curriculum of our children to provide this necessary support
ISBN 1 872767 56 7   25 pp   paperback   £3.95

The aims of school history: The National Curriculum and beyond
Peter Lee, John Slater, Paddy Walsh and John White with a preface by
Denis Shemilt

Why is it important to include history in the school curriculum? Is it because the subject (and its methodology) is so profoundly educative that it can be engaged in for its own sake? Or should the study of the past be harnessed to purposes such as preparation for democratic citizenship? These and other questions highlighted by the introduction of the National Curriculum are discussed here by historians and philosophers. The result is a lively and stimulating debate that has important implications for the future of school history.
ISBN 1 872767 26 5   55 pp   paperback   £4.50

Time to change the 1981 Education Act
Brahm Norwich

Brahm Norwich reviews the workings of the 1981 Education Act and how far the special education provision it was intended to enhance has been affected by the 1988 Education Act and subsequent developments. He argues for a reassessment of the definition of special educational need and for tightening the link between assessment of need and provision. Concern for the protection of provision on changing circumstances also prompts him to recommend that duties placed on local education authorities by the 1981 Act should be now extended to school governing bodies, and that parents should have the choice of a quicker form of decision making.
ISBN 1 872767 36 2   36 pp   paperback   £3.95

The promise and perils of educational comparison
Martin McLean

Can Britain's relatively poor economic performance be blamed on its inferior schools and teaching? Politicians in recent years have increasingly supported their proposals for educational reform with examples of practice in other countries. Against this background Martin McLean examines the uses and possible abuses of the discipline of comparative education. He illustrates his argument with many possible examples, concluding that the challenge to those who turn to other systems of education to find support for their arguments is whether they can let their thinking 'take in deeper and wider perspectives and whether they can accept the conclusions that emerge'.
ISBN 1 872767 31 1   40 pp   paperback   £3.95

National Curriculum science: So near and yet so far
Arthur Jennings

When the first proposals for the National Curriculum science were published in 1988 the goal of giving all pupils a broad and exciting experience of science seemed to be within reach. Arthur Jennings traces here the history of implementation and asks whether, under pressure of accommodating a workable system of assessment, that original goal has not been lost. Teachers will need to be vigilant, he urges, and carry parents and school governors with them, if they are to go beyond teaching 'to the tests' and achieve a real experience of science for all.
ISBN 1 872767 41 9   41 pp   paperback   £3.95

the Tufnell Press
47 Dalmeny Road,
London, N7 0DY

ORDER FORM

Please send me the following:

	Price	Quantity	Total

Total amount enclosed

Please make cheques payable to the Tufnell Press

NAME

ADDRESS

INS2/1994